A Marriage WITHOUT REGRETS

STUDY GUIDE

KAY ARTHUR

HARVEST HOUSE PUBLISHERS
Eugene, Oregon 97402

Cover by Koechel Peterson & Associates, Minneapolis, Minnesota

A MARRIAGE WITHOUT REGRETS
STUDY GUIDE
Copyright © 2000 by Kay Arthur
Published by Harvest House Publishers
Eugene, Oregon 97402

ISBN 0-7369-0439-5

Printed in the United States of America.

04   05   06   / BP-CF /   10   9   8   7   6

CONTENTS

Introduction

THIS STUDY GUIDE HIGHLIGHTS AND SUPPLEMENTS the excellent material in my book *A Marriage Without Regrets*. The lessons of this study guide correspond to the 14 chapters in the book to help prompt discussion, encourage reflection, and provide application of the main points.

Each lesson is divided into three main sections:

Looking Back

This section helps you review some of the main points covered in *A Marriage Without Regrets* by considering several comments from the book. Discussion questions are designed to promote a clearer understanding of where you are and where you want to be in your marriage and spiritual walk.

Looking Up

The heart of each study is a closer examination of the primary Scripture passages discussed in the main text. You'll read relevant portions of the Word of God and consider several questions about the meaning and application of the passages.

Looking Ahead

You are given several suggestions and insights about how to apply what you have learned in your study. Since the Word of God is "living and active and sharper than any two-edged sword" (see Hebrews 4:12), you'll want to take it out of its protective sheath and put it into dynamic action in your life. Application is the best way to accomplish that goal!

I pray that as you prayerfully work through each of these lessons you will find it a joy to "be diligent to present yourself approved to God as a workman who does not need to be ashamed, accurately handling the word of truth" (2 Timothy 2:15).

CHAPTER 1

A Marriage
Without Regrets

Looking Back

1. "All through my growing-up years, I had wanted only one thing: to be divinely in love, happily married, raise wonderful children, and live the good life."

   A. Do you think my childhood dream was unusual? Why or why not?

B. Did you grow up with dreams of what your marriage would be like? If so, describe them.

C. What expectations for marriage did you have after you became an adult? Where did these expectations come from?

2. "How quickly a lifetime of dreams can be deflated! We arrived in Bermuda on the second night of our honeymoon. And there in that idyllic setting, my new husband sat me down, looked me in the eyes, and said, 'Kay, you are now Mrs. Frank Thomas Goetz, Jr., and there are things I don't like about you. I want them changed.'"

A. How do you think you would have felt had you been me? Why?

B. What's the hardest part about seeing a dream deflated?

C. If you're married, what kind of dreams deflated for you after the wedding? When did these occur? How did you handle them?

D. How can we bring our deflated dreams to God?

3. "Each of us went into marriage with our own set of ideals and expectations without once bothering to find out what ideals, standards, and precepts *God* had set for the marriage relationship."

A. Why do you think Tom and I began our marriage without trying to find out God's ideals, standards, and precepts for our union?

B. Did you enter marriage (or are you entering it) by first discovering God's idea of it? Explain.

C. As you begin this study, list what you think are God's standards and precepts for marriage. What is most important to *Him?*

4. "God designed marriage to be a permanent, meaningful, truly fulfilling, and—yes—joyful relationship. Yet if we don't know His plans, if we haven't cried out for His counsel, we're likely to miss that fulfillment."

   A. What do each of the following terms mean in marriage? How are they lived out?

   • Permanent:

   • Meaningful:

   • Truly fulfilling:

- Joyful:

B. How have you sought to know God's plans for marriage? Have you cried out for His counsel? Explain.

C. What areas of your marriage seem less fulfilling than you'd hoped? How will knowing God's counsel on the subject help your relationship with your mate?

5. "The Bible will show you how to live in such a way that you will one day stand before Jesus Christ with no regrets in your heart. Come what may, you will have the confidence that you have lived in obedience and have done all that could be done to make your marriage a success."

A. Is it your goal to have a "marriage without regrets"? What would this mean for you?

B. How is obedience connected to having a marriage without regrets?

C. What does a successful marriage look like? How do you think you can achieve it?

Looking Up

1. Read Genesis 2:18-24.

A. According to this passage, what are God's expectations for marriage?

B. How do these compare to your own?

C. How can you reshape your expectations to fit God's expectations?

2. Read Genesis 3.

    A. How did the honeymoon end for Adam and Eve? What dreams of theirs were shattered?

    B. What can we learn from this tragic story that will help us build stronger marriages?

3. Read 2 Corinthians 7:10.

    A. What is the difference between "repentance" and "regret"?

    B. What kind of sorrow leads to repentance? What kind of sorrow leads to death?

C. Give an example of how godly sorrow in marriage can lead to repentance without regret.

D. Give an example of how worldly sorrow in marriage can lead to death.

E. What does this verse suggest about building a marriage without regrets?

Looking Ahead

1. List the concepts you have gleaned about building a marriage without regrets.

2. Write out any ideas you have held about marriage that don't seem to line up with God's Word.

3. Write out a prayer to God, telling Him specifically what you want to achieve in your marriage. Be sure to tell Him what you are willing to do to accomplish your desires. Remember: God loves to answer specific prayer (John 15:16)!

CHAPTER

Is It Possible to Live Happily Ever After?

Looking Back

1. "In all my dreaming and fantasizing, the emphasis was always on what I needed and what I wanted. 'As my needs and wants were met,' I told myself, 'I will respond to my mate accordingly.'"

   A. What problems can result from entering marriage with this kind of focus?

B. In what way is this kind of self-focus natural to all of us?

C. How can we overcome our natural bent toward self-centeredness, especially in marriage?

2. "In the long run, it doesn't matter how many books you've read, how many counselors you've consulted, or how many weekend conferences you've attended. What matters is this: Have you connected with the counsel in God's Word? Are you truly hearing Him? Are you obeying His precepts? Are you being guided by His Holy Spirit?"

A. How have you connected with God's counsel?

B. Are you truly listening to God?

C. Are you obeying His precepts?

D. Are you letting the Holy Spirit guide you?

E. Why is it so important to know and obey God's Word? Why can't human counselors give you equally good advice?

F. What has happened in your life when you have failed to heed God's Word? Describe some specific situations.

3. "Adam and Eve were to be God's vice-regents, co-rulers over all the earth. God gave this rulership not just to the man, but to the woman also. They were to reign side by side as partners. Woman was not less than man in God's eyes."

A. What does it mean to be a "vice-regent" or "co-ruler" over the earth? What kind of responsibility does this entail?

B. Why is it significant that God gave this rulership to Adam *and* Eve, and not merely to one or the other?

C. How can husbands show their wives that they understand that women aren't less than men in God's eyes?

4. "Woman was created *after* the man, she was created *for* the man, and she was created because it was *not good* for man to be alone. She was created as someone specially suitable for man...a helper."

   A. What is significant about the woman being created after the man?

   B. What is significant about the woman being created for the man?

   C. How did the creation of the woman correct the "not good" status of the man?

   D. What does it mean to be a "helper"? How does this fit with being a co-ruler?

5. "That old longing to 'live happily ever after' may not be a fairy tale after all. The precepts in God's timeless Word can enable us and empower us to reorder our lives and lift the shadow of regrets from our hearts."

   A. Do you think God's Word can show us a way to live "happily ever after" in marriage? If so, how? If not, why not?

B. How can God's Word help us reorder our married lives? Give at least one example.

C. How can God's Word keep us from years of regret? Give at least one example.

Looking Up

1. Read 2 Timothy 3:16,17.

A. According to verse 16, what is true of Scripture? What does "inspired" mean?

B. Name four areas in which Scripture is profitable to our lives.

C. According to verse 17, what is the goal of applying Scripture to our lives? What does this mean for your marriage?

2. Read Deuteronomy 8:3.

   A. According to this verse, what items are necessary to sustain life? How do we sometimes act as if this were not true?

   B. What does it mean to live "by everything that proceeds out of the mouth of the LORD"? Give at least one practical example from real life.

   C. How did Jesus respond to the very first temptation Satan offered as recorded in Matthew 4:1-4? What is significant about this for our lives?

3. Read Genesis 1:26-28.

   A. How were the man and woman created differently from all other creatures, according to these verses? How is that significant?

   B. To whom did God give the "rule" over every living thing on earth?

C. How is this passage especially important to building a solid home life? In what ways do we forget to take this passage into consideration?

4. Read Galatians 3:26-28.

A. According to verse 26, how does someone become a "son" of God?

B. What does it mean to be "clothed with Christ"?

C. For those who have become sons of God and are clothed with Christ, why are there no distinctions of personal worth between Jew and Greek, slave and free, male and female? What does this mean for marriage?

5. Read Genesis 2:18.

A. How was the woman "suitable" for the man?

B. How can a husband show his wife that he appreciates her help, recognizes her suitability for him, and honors her as his co-regent?

Looking Ahead

1. Together with your partner, plan a fun way to celebrate the co-regent status God has given the two of you. Design an activity that you both enjoy and that makes both of you feel like the royalty God says you are. Then do it this week!

2. Separately from your spouse, sit down with a pencil and a piece of paper and make a list of the following:

   - *Women:* Divide your paper into two columns. In one column, list the ways you enjoy being a "helper" to your husband. In the other column, list the ways you believe you could be more of a help to him.

   - *Men:* Divide your paper into two columns. In one column, list the things about your wife that make her "suitable" to you. In the other column, list the ways you believe you could better express your appreciation to her.

   When both lists are complete, sit down together and discuss what you've written. Make sure it's an encouraging time for both of you!

CHAPTER 3

What's the Glue That Holds a Marriage Together?

Looking Back

1. "When you look at another couple's marriage from afar—or even 'up close and personal'—it may seem far easier than it really is. Don't be deceived; marriage in our fallen world is not easy. It isn't easy even for those who belong to Jesus Christ and serve Him in some prominent way."

A. Why isn't marriage easy?

B. Is marriage easier for Christians? Why or why not?

2. "An intimate, daily walk with God is the most crucial element for holding a husband and wife and a family together. It is the most vital relationship in all of life—even more important than your relationship with your spouse or children, though they may be as dear to you as life itself."

A. Why is this daily walk so crucial for marriage?

B. How does this walk with God help a marriage thrive?

C. How would you describe your own walk with God?

3. "Through His death, Jesus Christ would deliver those who would believe in Him and receive Him as their God and Savior. They would be set free from Satan's dominion, from the one who held the power of death because of sin. It is only through Christ's sacrifice on the cross and His resurrection from the dead that they could be reconciled to God and experience the renewing of the Holy Spirit."

A. How did Jesus' death deliver believers from Satan's dominion?

B. What does it mean to be reconciled to God?

C. How can you tell if you have experienced the renewing of the Holy Spirit?

4. "[God] expects to be believed and obeyed, and He has given us the power to do so by giving us His Spirit. That life, that reliance, that obedience, is the glue that makes a marriage last in a day when marriages fall apart everywhere. It is a process of walking daily with God, knowing His Word, respecting Him, fearing Him, and obeying Him."

   A. How does the Holy Spirit help believers obey God? How does this work, practically speaking?

   B. What does it mean to respect God? To fear Him?

   C. How does knowing God's Word relate to obeying Him?

5. "Not only did God establish the marriage relationship with the principles of stewardship and identification built in, He also made it clear that this was a relationship that would have priority over all other relationships, with the exception of the relationship of a man or woman to God Himself."

   A. What is the principle of stewardship noted here?

B. What is the principle of identification noted here?

C. Why does marriage have priority over all other human relationships?

D. How are these principles lived out in your own experience?

Looking Up

1. Read Colossians 1:25-27.

A. What is the "mystery" Paul mentions in this passage?

B. Do you enjoy this "hope of glory"? Explain.

2. Read Psalm 56:11; 118:6; Hebrews 13:5,6.

A. What reason does the psalmist give in 56:11 for his lack of fear of man?

B. What reason does the psalmist give in 118:6 for his lack of fear?

C. What reason does the writer give in Hebrews 13:5,6 for his lack of fear? How does he encourage us to follow his example?

3. Read Matthew 16:24-27.

A. What does Jesus require of those who would follow Him? What does this mean?

B. How does one find life, according to Jesus?

C. Why does Jesus say the pursuit of God is the most important pursuit of all?

D. How should Jesus' return encourage us to grow in our faith?

4. Read John 14:23,24.

   A. According to this passage, what is an indicator of loving Jesus?

   B. What happens to those who obey Jesus' teaching?

   C. Why is it important to realize that Jesus' teaching comes from His Father?

Looking Ahead

1. Get a biography that details the married life of a well-known Christian couple from history (maybe *Martin Luther Had a Wife* or Billy Graham's *Just As I Am*). What struggles did this couple have to deal with? How did they manage? What can you learn from them? What encouragement can you take away? What errors can you avoid?

2. Many couples find it difficult to pray together. Is this an area of struggle in your marriage, or do you and your mate often pray together? Set aside half an hour today and get down on your knees with your spouse and pray about your marriage and family. Begin by praising God for the way He's already sustained and helped you, then detail specific prayer requests that you both agree are needed for a healthy home. End your time in thanksgiving that God is committed to you and your union.

CHAPTER 4

I Didn't Know Marriage Was Going to Be Like This!

Looking Back

1. "Sin is refusing to believe God and take Him at His Word."

   A. In what way is sin refusing to believe God?

   B. Is it possible to sin without rejecting God's Word? Explain.

2. "There was a twist in what Eve said—a slight distortion of God's Word that both hardened the prohibition and softened the consequences."

   A. What is the twist spoken of here?

   B. How can slight distortions of God's Word lead to major disasters?

   C. What's wrong with adding to God's command or taking away from His command?

3. "With one bite, sin entered the picture and their relationship with God shattered, as did their relationship with one another."

   A. What was so bad about taking a bite out of a piece of fruit?

   B. How does sin shatter your relationship to God?

C. How does sin shatter your relationship to your spouse?

4. "The key to a marriage without regrets is first and foremost a living, moment-by-moment relationship with God through the Lord Jesus Christ."

    A. Why is a vital relationship to God the key to marriage?

    B. How can you begin a vital relationship with God?

    C. How can you strengthen a vital relationship with God?

Looking Up

1. Read Genesis 3:1-19.

    A. Why was it so important for the serpent to first cast doubt on what God had said?

B. Why do you think God's command was altered in Eve's reply?

C. Adam and Eve's sin resulted in many dire consequences. List as many as possible.

D. In your view, what was the worst consequence of sin? Why?

2. Read Romans 5:12-14.

A. How did sin enter the world, according to Paul?

B. What resulted from the entrance of sin into the world?

3. Read Romans 5:8; 10:9-12.

   A. How did God deal with the problem of sin?

   B. How do we appropriate God's work on our behalf, according to Romans 10?

   C. Have you entered into a new relationship with God through Jesus? Explain.

4. Read Romans 8:1; 2 Corinthians 5:17.

   A. How can we avoid being condemned, according to Romans 8:1? What does it mean to be "in Christ"?

   B. How does being "in Christ" make us new creations? How does this affect all of life?

Looking Ahead

1. Sin is not merely a theological concept, but it's also an unwelcome reality in all of our homes. Try this exercise sometime when you both are up for it. Set aside some time one evening when you're both energetic and positive. Find the courage to ask your spouse to name the five things you do that irritate him or her the most. It might be best to take turns. Bathe this evening in prayer, and remember Paul's guidance to "speak the truth in love." The idea is not to have a gripe session, but to identify (and then take steps to eliminate) the recurring rough spots in your marriage. Make sure to reaffirm your love for one another.

2. If you have never done so, write out in two or three pages how the Lord rescued you from your sin and brought you into His kingdom. Then ask your spouse to read your story so that you can rejoice together in God's goodness.

CHAPTER 5

What Does God Expect of the Husband?

Looking Back

1. "Of all the words used for love, *agape* is the noblest. It's the word God uses to describe His love for you. It's the kind of love you have always longed for in your mom, your dad, your wife, your child."

A. How would you describe God's love for you?

B. Describe the kind of love you've always longed for.

C. How would you define *agape* love to someone who has never heard of it? How would you demonstrate it to that person?

2. "A husband is commanded to continuously love his wife *in and of herself, regardless of who she is or what she does.*"

A. How can a husband love his wife "in and of herself"?

B. When is it hard to love someone regardless of who she is or what she does?

C. Why does God command such love?

3. A husband should love his wife "just as Christ loved the church" and "as he loves his own body."

   A. How did Christ love the church? Describe how He treated her.

   B. How do men love their own bodies? Describe what they do.

   C. In what practical ways do these two pictures help a husband know how to love his wife?

4. "How can you practically encourage your wife today? How can you show her this *agape* love? How can you minister to her needs?"

   A. How will you encourage your wife today?

   B. What needs does your wife have that you can meet right now?

C. How do you think your wife would like to receive *agape* love from you?

Looking Up

1. Read Ephesians 5:25-33.

A. How did Christ give Himself up for the church? Why did He do this?

B. How are husbands to follow Christ's example?

C. Why does Paul say that "he who loves his own wife loves himself"?

D. In your own words, what does the idea of "one flesh" between husband and wife mean?

2. Read Colossians 3:19.

   A. How is Paul's instruction in this verse similar to that in Ephesians 5? How is it different?

   B. Why do you think Paul emphasizes that husbands should not be embittered against their wives?

3. Read 1 Peter 3:7.

   A. How does Peter instruct husbands to treat their wives?

   B. Why are husbands to show their wives respect?

   C. How does your marriage affect your prayer life?

Looking Ahead

1. Women thrive on the little things that their men do for them. Husbands, when was the last time you:

   - Complimented her on the way she keeps house?

   - Thanked her for keeping you in clean clothes?

   - Told her that a meal was good?

   - Praised her for the way she handles the children?

   - Brought home a rose or bouquet for no special reason?

   - Showed her how neat it is to have her for your wife?

   - Sent her a "mushy" card?

   - Made a big deal out of her birthday?

2. May I recommend an excellent book for you men? The book is a classic: James C. Dobson's *What Wives Wish Their Husbands Knew About Women* (Tyndale House Publishers, Inc.). It will be well worth the time it takes to read it!

CHAPTER 6

I'M A WOMAN!
WHAT IS MY VALUE?

Looking Back

1. "It's when we refuse to embrace the truth of our gender differences (and all they imply) that our society begins to tear apart at the seams."

A. What important differences are there between the genders?

B. Why does our society refuse to embrace the truth?

C. Give an example from your own experience of what happens when people refuse to see a difference between the sexes.

2. "It is clear that God ordained the man to rule over the woman. Therefore, for a wife to declare her 'independence' from her husband's headship is to fight against the wisdom, will, and choice of Elohim, our Creator."

A. What does it mean that the man is to rule over the woman? What does it not mean?

B. How can a wife "declare her independence from her husband's headship" without ever saying those words?

C. Why do you think God made the man "head" over the woman?

3. "Should a husband force his wife to submit? Please note that the Scripture tells a woman to subject herself. The passage says nothing about husbands compelling their wives to submit."

   A. How do some husbands try to force their wives to submit to them?

   B. What difference does it make if a wife submits to her husband voluntarily or under compulsion?

4. "It may be traditional for a man to make all the decisions in your family, but it is not biblical. And it doesn't even make good common sense. Remember, husbands, your wives are your counterparts, your completers. You need them. A wise and prudent man won't move independently of his wife."

   A. Who makes the decisions in your family?

B. How are decisions made?

C. How can husbands and wives make sound decisions together?

5. "How quick are you to let your man know he's appreciated and valued? When was the last time you thanked him for bringing home a paycheck (regular or not)?"

A. How does your husband most like to be appreciated and valued?

B. What actions do not communicate that you value and appreciate your husband?

C. What will you do this week to let your mate know you appreciate him?

Looking Up

1. Read Genesis 1:26,27.

   A. Of what significance is the fact that both the man and the woman were made in the image of God?

   B. Why did God give rule over the earth to both man and woman?

2. Read 1 Corinthians 11:3,7-9,11,12.

   A. What does it mean that the husband is the "head" of the woman? What does it not mean?

   B. Why is it important to know that the woman was created for the man? Why is it important that men are born of women?

C. How does this passage show the differences between and the equality of the sexes?

3. Read Ephesians 5:22-24,33.

A. How are wives supposed to relate to their husbands? Why?

B. Define "submission" in your own words: What does it mean? What does it not mean?

C. How is "respect" different from submission (see verse 33)? How is it related?

4. Read Colossians 3:18.

A. How are wives to relate to their husbands, according to this passage?

B. What reason is given for this command? What does this mean?

5. Read 1 Peter 3:1-6.

A. How does Peter tell wives to relate to their husbands?

B. What reasons does he give?

C. Why does Peter warn against giving way to "fear" (see verse 6)?

Looking Ahead

1. You may not believe it, but men are incurable romantics. Admire and respect your husband this week by:

   - Writing love notes. Send them to his office, put them in his lunch sack, pin them to his underwear or pajamas when he travels, put them on the bathroom mirror.

   - Squeezing or noticing his muscles.

- Commending him for the way he handles the children.

- Pursuing his affections some evening so that he knows he is respected, wanted, and needed.

- Admiring something he has just done.

2. To see the high value Jesus placed on women, read through the Gospel of Luke, noticing how the roles of women are highlighted and emphasized throughout the book. As you read, ask yourself these questions: How did Jesus treat women? How did women assist Him in His ministry? Where and in what circumstances were women specifically mentioned? Now ask and answer: How does Jesus view me? How do I fit into His current plan and purpose?

CHAPTER

Your Home: A Little Bit of Heaven?

Looking Back

1. "Our goal in marriage and in establishing our homes ought to be to bring to earth a little heaven—a picture of our spiritual family in the heavenly home that awaits us."

   A. In what ways have you tasted heaven in your home?

B. How is your home supposed to be a picture of God's home in heaven?

C. Does this idea encourage or frustrate you? Explain.

2. "Heaven...is a place of safety and security. A place of love, joy, peace, and total acceptance. Is that what it's like in your home?"

A. How is your home a place of safety and security? In what ways could it improve in these areas?

B. Would you say your home is a place of love, joy, peace, and total acceptance? Explain.

C. What would help you create a home that feels more like heaven?

3. "A man's esteem generally comes from the workplace, while a woman's is found in her husband and her children."

   A. Do you agree with this statement? Why or why not?

   B. Why is the workplace generally so important to a man?

   C. Why is the home generally so important to a woman?

   D. Are these generalizations true of your own experience? Explain.

Looking Up

1. Read Ephesians 3:14,15.

   A. What comes to mind when you think of God's heavenly family?

   B. What does it mean that we derive our "name" from our heavenly Father?

   C. How are our homes to reflect our Father's home?

2. Read 1 Timothy 5:8.

   A. In what way is a man to provide for his family?

   B. How important is this task?

C. In what way is a Christian man who refuses to provide for his family worse than an unbeliever?

3. Read 1 Timothy 5:14.

A. What counsel does Paul give to younger widows? Why does he give this counsel?

B. What does it mean to "keep house"? What does this entail?

4. Read Titus 2:3-5.

A. How can someone be reverent in the way they live? Why is this the first instruction here?

B. What kind of instruction are older women to give younger women? List the various elements of this instruction.

C. What happens when these instructions are not followed (verse 5)?

5. Read Proverbs 31.

A. How does this passage provide a picture of Titus 2:3-5?

B. How does this passage show that submission does not mean loss of strong personality?

Looking Ahead

1. Just for fun, why don't you do something special for your mate that expresses your love for him or her in the language of love that he or she understands? Don't make a big deal out of it; just do it quietly, lovingly, and see what happens!

2. Try an experiment this week. Think only good, pleasing thoughts about your mate. Any time a negative thought enters your mind, cast it out and refuse to dwell on it.

CHAPTER

WHAT HAPPENED TO LOVE?

Looking Back

1. "New Testament Greek uses four different words for 'love.'"

- *Storge,* the love of natural affection.
- *Eros,* the love of passion.
- *Phileo,* the "I really care for you" love.
- *Agape,* the love without limit.

A. Define in your own terms the meaning of each of these words for love.

B. When you think of love, which of these four types usually comes to mind? Why?

C. Who in your life has most shown you *agape* love? Describe what he or she did.

2. "Unconditional love never gives up. It digs in and continues to love despite hardship or disappointment and right in the face of apathy, anger, frustration, and failure....*Agape* chooses to love, no matter what."

A. When is it hardest for you to show *agape* love to your children? To your spouse?

B. When do you most need to receive *agape* love?

C. Describe a time when someone showed you *agape* love despite your behavior.

3. "Meaningful rituals and gestures of love can go a long way in your marriage. The hello and good-bye kisses, the hugs…the tender secrets…all serve to make your relationship more special."

   A. Name several examples of this in your own marriage.

   B. Name some examples of this you have seen in the marriages of others you know.

   C. What rituals or gestures of love could you use to show your mate how special he or she is to you?

4. "The unconditional love God showed us is the very same love we're to show our spouses."

   A. Is it possible to show God's *agape* love to our spouses? Explain.

   B. What do you do when you don't *feel* like showing God's kind of love?

C. How can you show God's kind of love to your spouse this evening?

Looking Up

1. Read Jeremiah 31:3; John 3:16.

   A. With what kind of love did God love His people, according to Jeremiah?

   B. How did God show His love to the world, according to John?

   C. How does God's kind of love affect you personally?

2. Read 1 John 4:10,11; John 15:13.

   A. What effect should God's love for us have on our relationship with others?

   B. According to Jesus, what is the ultimate expression of our love?

3. Read 1 Corinthians 13.

   A. Why does Paul call this "the most excellent way" (1 Corinthians 12:31)?

   B. How would you summarize the apostle's teaching on love, as presented here?

   C. What elements of this kind of love are the most difficult for you to express? Which are the easiest?

   D. Why is love greater than faith and hope?

4. Read Romans 5:5.

   A. In what way does godly hope not disappoint us?

B. How does this verse assure us that believers have within them the power to show God's love to others?

Looking Ahead

1. Write out a definition of the kind of love that you ought to have for your marriage partner. Be honest with yourself and ask, "Do I really have this love for my partner?" If the answer is no, what steps can you take to start loving in this way?

2. Get out a sheet of paper and write down the fun rituals you have and wish you had in marriage. The two columns should look like this:

Rituals we have: *Rituals I'd like to have:*

Show your spouse this list after you're finished, then discuss how you could both act on individual items.

CHAPTER 9

COMMUNICATION: THE GREAT PRIORITY

Looking Back

1. "Communication is the art of listening, watching, and sharing.... It is the free exchange of thoughts, ideas, and opinions shared between two or more people who are willing to be open, honest, and yes, vulnerable."

   A. How good are you at listening? At watching? At sharing?

B. How willing are you to be open with your mate? How willing are you to be honest with your mate? How willing are you to be vulnerable with your mate? Explain.

C. On a scale of 1 to 10 (1 = poor, 10 = excellent), how would you rate your communication with your spouse? Explain.

2. "If only we could remember just this much in our marriages! We all stumble. Every one of us. And we do so in a million ways. None of us is perfect. We all make mistakes and fall short, even of our own ideals."

A. Why would remembering this single principle revolutionize many marriages?

B. How easy is it for you to remember this principle when your spouse messes up?

C. Do you struggle with perfectionism? Does your spouse? How does this affect your marriage?

3. "[Let's] look at four essential factors of marriage that must be in place before good communication can happen. If you work at these four essentials, they'll provide a solid basis for positive communication that leads to a strong, healthy marriage":

   • Uphold the priority of your marriage.

   • Uphold the permanence of your marriage.

   • Uphold the oneness of your marriage.

   • Uphold the openness of your marriage.

   A. How can you uphold the priority of your marriage?

   B. How can you uphold the permanence of your marriage?

   C. How can you uphold the oneness of your marriage?

D. How can you uphold the openness of your marriage?

E. Rate yourself from 1 to 10 (1 = poor, 10 = excellent) in each of these areas. Where do you need the most work? What can you do to improve?

4. "We need to constantly evaluate and work on our communication skills.... Here are a few I've been working on":

- Learn to communicate with your eyes.
- Give the gift of your full attention.
- Respond when someone speaks to you.
- Keep a confidence.
- Avoid pat answers.
- Allow your mate to open up about his or her fears.
- Continually look for ways to build your mate's self-esteem.
- When you talk, don't attack!
- Never, never let the sun go down on your wrath.
- The word "divorce" should never be in your vocabulary.

A. Which of the tips on the previous page do you most struggle with? Explain.

B. Which of these tips come most naturally to you? How does it help your marriage?

C. Are any of these tips currently not in your marriage toolbox? What can you do to add them and use them?

Looking Up

1. Read James 3:2-12.

A. How is the tongue like a bit in a horse's mouth? How is it like a ship's rudder?

B. How is the tongue like a fire?

C. Why is it so difficult to tame the tongue?

D. What is the only way the tongue can be tamed? In other words, how do we turn it into a fresh-water spring?

2. Read Ephesians 4:29-31; 5:4,19,20.

A. What does Paul mean by "unwholesome talk"?

B. What kind of communication is helpful and builds others up?

C. How should our communication be tailored to the needs of others?

D. What should we avoid, according to 5:4? What should we practice?

E. How can 5:19,20 instruct our communication with our spouse?

3. Read Job 16:4,5.

A. What contrast is made in this passage?

B. What did Job choose to do?

C. How can we follow his example?

4. Read Proverbs 10:19; 11:13; 12:18,25; 13:3; 15:1,4,23,30.

A. What do you learn about communication from these texts?

B. Which of these verses speaks the loudest to you? Why?

Looking Ahead

1. The book of Proverbs contains scores of insights into godly communication. Scan the book, and note every verse that deals with healthy speech. When you're finished, go back over your list and spend more extended time with these verses. What did you learn from your study? What can you put into practice immediately?

2. I highly recommend that you write Chuck and Barb Snyder, P.O. Box 819, Edmonds, Washington, 98020-0819, and ask them how you can purchase their audio series on communication called "Accepting Differences." It is outstanding and the most helpful series on the subject that Jack and I know of!

CHAPTER 10

SEX...GOD'S WAY

Looking Back

1. "Sex was to be the first item on the first couple's agenda—even higher in priority than their oversight of the world."

   A. Why do you think God made sex a priority over vocation?

   B. Why do you think God designed sex in the way He did?

C. God made some plants and animals asexual. Why do you think He made humans sexual beings?

2. "If you can do anything to make yourself more attractive to your husband (and do it in a healthy way without harming yourself), then choose your course and start today."

   A. What sorts of things does your husband find most attractive in you?

   B. How could you make yourself more physically attractive to your mate?

3. "One of the most common reasons that believers may struggle with enjoyment of sex is the sense of guilt that arises from immoral sexual activity in their pasts."

   A. Do you agree with this statement? Why or why not?

B. If you have had to deal with sexual guilt from your past, how have you handled it?

C. How can we be free from *all* guilt over a sinful past?

4. "Abstinence should only come by mutual agreement, and then only for a reasonable amount of time. The purpose for abstinence should be for extended prayer, period."

A. What is a "reasonable amount of time," in your opinion?

B. Why is abstinence appropriate for extended prayer?

Looking Up

1. Read Proverbs 5:15-19.

A. How does this passage encourage married couples to enjoy physical intimacy with each other?

B. How does it instruct them to keep sex only within marriage?

C. How can you make sure that both of you will be ever-captivated by your love for each other?

2. Read 1 Corinthians 6:9-20; 1 Thessalonians 4:3-8.

A. What instructions does the apostle give in these passages regarding sexual conduct?

B. Why do you think Paul speaks so strongly on this subject? Why is it so important?

3. Read 1 Corinthians 7:1-5.

   A. How is marriage supposed to avoid the lure of immorality?

   B. What instruction does Paul give in verse 3?

   C. What reason for this instruction does Paul give in verse 4?

   D. Note that verse 5 speaks of "agreement." Why is this crucial?

Looking Ahead

1. Sit down with your spouse some evening, away from kids, and read the Song of Solomon to each other. Turn down the lights and read by candlelight, if possible. Use a translation, such as the NASB,

that includes subheads showing who is speaking. Take turns reading aloud, the wife reading the part of the Bride, the husband the part of Solomon (Bridegroom). Enjoy!

2. Get a copy of Ed Wheat's book *Love Life for Every Married Couple*. Read chapters 3 and 6. Record any insights you find particularly helpful or challenging.

CHAPTER 11

RAISING GODLY CHILDREN: WHERE DO YOU BEGIN?

Looking Back

1. "The best and most important and loving thing you can do for your children is to build a strong, stable marriage with your spouse. Nothing apart from Christ is more important."

A. Describe your parents' marriage. Was it strong?

B. Why is a loving marriage the bedrock for raising godly children?

C. Do your children know you love your spouse? Explain.

2. "Kids need to have Mom and Dad around. Available. Reachable. Touchable. Accessible!"

A. How much time do you spend with your kids every day?

B. Can your kids approach you when they need you? Explain.

C. What do these words mean to you: available, reachable, touchable, accessible?

3. "I believe you should do everything you can to have mother at home when the children are at home."

   A. Do you agree with this statement? Why or why not?

   B. Why is it so important to have mother at home?

   C. What changes would you have to make to be at home for your kids? How workable are these changes? Explain.

4. "Let your children hear you pray for them individually at the breakfast table."

   A. How often do your children hear you pray for them by name?

B. What would you like to pray in the hearing of your children? (Remember—prayer is to God, not to the kids!)

Looking Up

1. Read Psalm 127.

A. How can you invite the Lord to help you build your house?

B. How does God see children, according to verse 3?

C. How do verses 4 and 5 picture a parent's relationship to children in older age?

2. Read Psalm 139:13-16.

   A. How can this passage give children a tremendous confidence in life?

   B. How can verse 16, especially, give encouragement in difficult times?

3. Read Ephesians 5:15,16.

   A. Are you careful with the way you are building your family? Explain.

   B. Are you making the most of every opportunity to raise godly children? In what ways?

   C. Do you think our days are "evil"? Explain.

D. Why is it especially important to make the most of every opportunity when the days are evil?

Looking Ahead

1. If you have children living at home, create a chart like the following and record the information called for in each column of the chart. (By "temperament," I mean quiet/active; moody/cheerful; relaxed/nervous; introvert/extrovert; and so on.)

Child	Strengths	Weaknesses	Interests	Temperament

In the light of the chart, list what you see as each child's personal needs.

2. For a helpful, encouraging book on the ultimate goal of parenting, get a copy of *Gifts from God* by Dr. David Jeremiah. This book, written by a seasoned pastor, father, and grandfather, should lift your spirits and give you encouragement to press on.

CHAPTER 12

RAISING GODLY CHILDREN: OUR HOPE AND RESPONSIBILITY

Looking Back

1. "The best way to communicate with your children is not to sit them down for a lecture, but rather to let truth flow from your conversation as you drive, do a project together…or sit together on the bed at night." Teach your children to obey you and to honor you.

   A. How do you teach your children to obey you?

B. How do you teach your children to honor you?

C. What's the difference between obeying and honoring?

2. "Exhortation calls our children to the next level and encourages them even when it must gently rebuke them. It says things like, 'Oh, son, listen to me. That kind of behavior isn't worthy of you. That is beneath you. You don't need to do that. You don't want to behave that way!' And then it paints a compelling picture of what our children can become."

A. How can you best exhort your children? How does your exhortation differ from child to child?

B. Is gentle rebuke easy or hard for you? Explain.

C. What sorts of pictures are you painting for your own children about what they can become?

3. "When Proverbs 22:6 instructs parents to 'train up a child in the way he should go,' it's talking about setting a child on God's pathway to life." Here are three things to keep in mind when you discipline your children:

- Understand their bent.

- Consider their uniqueness.

- Honor their individuality.

A. Describe the "bent" of each of your children.

B. How do you take the uniqueness of your children into account in the way you discipline them? Encourage them?

C. How can you better honor the individuality of each of your children?

4. "To discipline our children is to regulate their behavior, to show them what is right and wrong, to teach them the importance of setting God-honoring goals. What are they to live for? What really has value? More important than anything else, we're to point them to the eternal."

A. What specific methods do you employ to regulate the behavior of your children?

B. Do your children know why they're living? What do they think really has value?

C. How are you teaching your children the vital significance of eternal things?

5. "Proverbs 22:6 is not a promise. It is simply a statement about how life normally turns out when we live in a certain way. Normally it comes true...but not always."

   A. Why is it important to realize that Proverbs 22:6 is not a promise?

   B. If Proverbs 22:6 is not a promise, then what hope can it give us as parents?

Looking Up

1. Read Proverbs 22:6.

   A. How are you training your children? What does this involve specifically?

   B. Describe the way you want your children to go. What does this look like?

2. Read Ephesians 6:1-4.

   A. Why are children instructed to obey their parents?

   B. What promise is connected to obeying one's parents?

   C. What kinds of things provoke your children? How can these be avoided?

   D. Describe the "instruction of the Lord" that you are giving your children. Are you satisfied with this? Explain.

3. Read Deuteronomy 6:1-9.

   A. What ideas does this passage give on instructing our children?

B. In what kinds of things are we to instruct our children, according to this passage?

4. Read Judges 6:1-16.

A. What situation confronted Israel and Gideon in this passage?

B. How did God give Gideon a vision for his future?

C. How can we do something similar for our own children?

5. Read Proverbs 13:24; 19:18; 22:15; 23:13,14; 29:15,17.

A. What do these verses teach you about the discipline of children?

B. Describe your own views on child discipline. How are they influenced by the Bible?

Looking Ahead

1. Build memories for your children. One of the greatest times as a family comes around the dinner table. Sometimes it may seem like a three-ring circus, but enjoy the laughs! Establish significant rituals—things the children can count on happening, especially at holidays. Do this even in the teenage years, when it may seem "dumb" to continue. When your kids hit their twenties, they'll reminisce about it all—probably at the dinner table.

2. Consider making a "Family Development Notebook." Set some specific goals of traits you would like to see developed in each individual of your family (including yourself). Having specific goals helps you determine how and where you are going to spend your time and your money. List some goals for your family's spiritual life. Writing down your goals and planning ways to meet them will not only help you develop your family in a consistent way, but goals and plans will also help you evaluate your progress.

CHAPTER 13

GOD HELP US...
IT'S MONEY AGAIN!

Looking Back

1. "Marriage counselors tell us that money is one of the major causes of marital strife. When a husband and wife cannot agree on how to handle their money, their disagreements will eventually spill over into other areas of their relationship—and the fighting all too often ends up in divorce court."

   A. Why do you think money issues are often so volatile in a family?

B. How do you handle finances in your marriage?

C. What financial issues most often lead to arguments or strife in your marriage?

2. "[Here are] two fundamentals that will hold you through any financial crisis":

   • God is the source of all things.

   • God is the provider of all things.

   A. How does remembering that God is the source of all things help in a financial crisis?

   B. How does remembering that God is the provider of all things help in a financial crisis?

   C. Why do you think God wants us to remember these two fundamentals?

3. "Where's your heart? Where do you spend your time, energy, and money? Either you've made God the focal point of your life or your affections are set upon the things of this earth. Both cannot be true at the same time."

A. Write out the answers to the questions posed above.

B. Describe a good test to determine where someone's heart lies.

C. Why is it impossible to set your affections upon both God and the things of this earth?

4. "A major way to grant [a wife] the honor she deserves is to include her in financial decision-making. Many a man could be saved from a bad business deal by consulting his wife and trusting God to move them jointly toward a wise decision."

A. How are financial decisions made in your home? Are you satisfied with this process? Explain.

B. Why do many men seem fearful of asking for the input of their wives on financial matters?

C. Describe a time when God moved you and your spouse toward a joint financial decision.

5. "In general, the New Testament pattern for giving is giving generously and cheerfully to support God's work and His people. The Lord has entrusted us with His riches so that we might use them for His kingdom. Beyond that, the New Testament suggests several other ways we should give":

- Give regularly.
- Give to those who minister to you.
- Give to widows and the poor.
- Give what is due to the government.

A. Are you satisfied with your current giving patterns? Explain.

B. Why do you think God instructs us to give in the ways just outlined?

C. In what way is our use of money a good barometer of our spiritual maturity?

Looking Up

1. Read 1 Samuel 2:7,8; James 1:17.

   A. What does God have to do with human poverty? Human wealth?

   B. How does God humble someone financially? How does He exalt someone else?

C. From where do all good things come? Why is this important to remember?

2. Read Matthew 6:19-21,24-33.

A. What do verses 19-21 tell us to do? What do they tell us to avoid? How is it obvious which road we have chosen?

B. Why does Jesus tell us it is foolish to worry about finances?

C. In what way do some believers live as though they didn't know God?

D. In practical terms, what does it mean to seek God's kingdom?

3. Read Proverbs 10:4,5; 2 Thessalonians 3:11,12.

   A. Does refusing to worry about finances mean that we should do nothing about them? Explain.

   B. How does a person's attitude toward work help to indicate the depth of his or her walk with God?

4. Read 1 Timothy 6:5-10.

   A. What does Paul say is wrong with believing that godliness is a means to financial gain?

   B. What ought to be the Christian's attitude toward money and finances?

   C. How is verse 10 often misquoted? How can pursuit of money devastate human lives?

5. Read 2 Corinthians 8–9.

   A. What principles about giving do you glean from this extended passage?

   B. Why do you think Paul refuses to command the Corinthians about their giving?

   C. In what way is Jesus our ultimate example of giving (8:9)?

Looking Ahead

1. If you struggle with finances in your family, it might be wise to get more counsel. Two of the most trustworthy Christian counselors in this arena are Larry Burkett and Ron Blue. Both have published numerous books on the subject and provide helpful, practical advice on how to get a handle on this difficult issue.

2. Take a close look at the entries in your checkbook over the past year. What does it tell you about your patterns of giving to church, Christian ministries which give you help, charities, and people in need? As a couple, discuss your findings and determine whether any changes need to be made.

CHAPTER 14

WHAT GOD HAS JOINED TOGETHER

Looking Back

1. "We don't have to wonder how God feels about divorce, do we? He hates it. The Hebrew word for marriage is *kiddushin,* which means 'consecration, sanctification, set apart unto God.' The Hebrew concept of marriage, then, is being set apart unto one another. God is angered by those who say there's nothing wrong with divorce. He made marriage a permanent covenant for the sake of protecting the family and bringing up godly offspring."

A. Why does God hate divorce?

B. If God so hates divorce, why did He allow it?

C. If divorce has touched you or your family, describe its effects.

2. "According to Jesus, then, adultery is legitimate grounds for divorce. Does that mean that divorce ought to happen automatically after adultery? Certainly not."

A. Why is adultery legitimate grounds for divorce?

B. Why is divorce not *required* because of adultery?

C. How is God able to heal a marriage scarred by adultery? How can we help rather than hinder the process?

3. "If the unbeliever wants a divorce, Scripture allows it. The believer in that case is free to remarry—but only to another believer."

   A. Why does God allow divorce in the case of an unbeliever who abandons the marriage?

   B. Is divorce allowable if the spouse who abandons the marriage professes to be a believer? Explain.

   C. Why is remarriage allowed only to another believer?

4. "So often people want to know if God allows divorce or remarriage under any circumstances other than death, adultery, or desertion. I know this sounds hard, but I know of no other biblical reasons. Quite frankly, it all comes down to a matter of obedience to the clear teaching of God's Word—and the desire to please God above all else."

A. Why do you think God's Word allows no other reason for divorce other than death, adultery, or desertion?

B. How would you counsel a person who is married to an abusive spouse?

C. How would you respond to the person who says, "Well, God wants me to be happy. This divorce will make me happy. Therefore God wants me to get this divorce"?

Looking Up

1. Read Malachi 2:13-16.

A. What does it mean that someone has "dealt treacherously" with his or her spouse?

B. From these verses, why does God hate divorce?

2. Read Deuteronomy 24:1-4.

A. What specific case of divorce and remarriage is discussed in this passage?

B. Why is someone not allowed to remarry a former partner who in the intervening time has been married to someone else?

3. Read Matthew 19:3-9.

A. Why does Jesus begin His answer to the question of divorce by discussing what marriage was intended to be?

B. What is the only reason for divorce that Jesus gives in this passage?

4. Read 1 Corinthians 7:10-16,39.

   A. What is Paul's general rule about divorce?

   B. If a believer gets a divorce contrary to the Bible's instructions, is he or she free to remarry?

   C. How should a believer act toward an unbelieving spouse?

   D. Why do you think God is so concerned that marriages remain intact?

Looking Ahead

1. It surprises many individuals to discover that God Himself has been divorced. Read Ezekiel 16 and Jeremiah 2:1–3:18. What do

you learn about this sad incident? How does God follow His own law on marriage and divorce?

2. Read the book of Hosea to get an idea of how God feels emotionally when a marriage falls apart. How does this knowledge encourage you to redouble your efforts to keep your own marriage strong?

Precept Ministries International

Precept Ministries International is a year-round Bible study and conference center dedicated to establishing God's people in God's Word. If you would like to know more about Kay Arthur or Precept Ministries, please write or call:

Precept Ministries International
P.O. Box 182218
Chattanooga, TN 37422-7218

(423) 892-6814

HARVEST HOUSE BOOKS
BY KAY ARTHUR

ᔕᔕᔕᔕ

God, Are You There?
Speak to My Heart, God
God, Help Me Experience More of You
How to Study Your Bible
Israel, My Beloved
Just a Moment with You, God
Lord, Teach Me to Pray in 28 Days
A Marriage Without Regrets
A Marriage Without Regrets Study Guide
With an Everlasting Love

Bibles
The New Inductive Study Bible (NASB)

Discover 4 Yourself®
Inductive Bible Studies for Kids
How to Study Your Bible for Kids
Lord, Teach Me to Pray for Kids
God's Amazing Creation (Genesis 1–2)
Digging Up the Past (Genesis 3–11)
Abraham—God's Brave Explorer (Genesis 11–25)
Joseph—God's Superhero (Genesis 37–50)
Wrong Way, Jonah! (Jonah)
Jesus in the Spotlight (John 1–11)
Jesus—Awesome Power, Awesome Love (John 11–16)
Jesus—To Eternity and Beyond! (John 17–21)
Boy, Have I Got Problems! (James)
God, What's Your Name?

New Inductive Study Series
Teach Me Your Ways (Genesis, Exodus,Leviticus, Numbers, Deuteronomy)
Choosing Victory, Overcoming Defeat (Joshua, Judges, Ruth)
Desiring God's Own Heart (1 & 2 Samuel, 1 Chronicles)
Come Walk in My Ways (1 & 2 Kings, 2 Chronicles)
Overcoming Fear and Discouragement (Ezra, Nehemiah, Esther)
Trusting God in Times of Adversity (Job)
God's Blueprint for Bible Prophecy (Daniel)
Opening the Windows of Blessings (Haggai, Zechariah, Malachi)
The Call to Follow Jesus (Luke)
The Holy Spirit Unleashed in You (Acts)
God's Answers for Relationships and Passions (1 & 2 Corinthians)
Free from Bondage God's Way (Galatians, Ephesians)
That I May Know Him (Philippians, Colossians)
Standing Firm in These Last Days (1 & 2 Thessalonians)
Walking in Power, Love, and Discipline (1 & 2 Timothy, Titus)
Living with Discernment in the End Times (1 & 2 Peter, Jude)
Behold, Jesus Is Coming! (Revelation)